Friends
are cheaper than therapy

This book is for all my wonderful friends all over the world.

This edition first published in the United Kingdom in 2015 by
Portico
43 Great Ormond Street
London
WC1N 3HZ

An imprint of Pavilion Books Company Ltd

Sterling Publishing Co., Inc.
1166 Avenue of the Americas, 17th floor
New York, NY 10036

ISBN 978-1-90939-637-1

A CIP catalogue record for this book is available from the British Library.

12 11

Design: Suzanne Perkins/grafica
Colour reproduction by Rival Colour Ltd, UK
Printed and bound by Toppan Leefung Printing Ltd, China
This book can be ordered direct from the publisher at www.pavilionbooks.com

THE WIT AND
Cath Tate
WISDOM OF

Friends

are cheaper than therapy

PORTICO

Between
me and insanity
stand my
friends.

A friend is someone with whom you can be yourself.

A friend
is someone
who likes you
even though they
know you.

A good friend is cheaper than therapy.

Friends are
God's apology
for relatives.

Friends are the most reliable insurance policy.

A friend is
someone you can go out
clubbing with.

A best friend sometimes has four legs.

Outside of a dog,
a book is a
man's best friend.

Inside of a dog,
it's too dark to read.

Sometimes your friends seem just *too* familiar.

Some friends just love a disaster.

People who are late
are always so much jollier
than their friends
who have to wait!

Some friends are lively, witty, vivacious…

…and always forgetting their keys.

But who needs friends
when you've got style?

"It's being so cheerful that keeps me going."

Some people are just born to be wild.

Our book club can beat up
your book club.

Nobody knows
where I keep my hip flask.

Life without cake is possible…

.…but pointless.

Life's too short to be thin.

"It's great being a therapist.
I just love the gossip."

Women talk a lot
even when no one
is listening.

Men talk a lot
even when they have
nothing to say.

It's better if men don't know
what women talk about.

Your greatest fear –
there is no PMT, this is just
your personality.

"We didn't know how unhappy we were until we had therapy!"

“Even my imaginary friend
doesn't listen to me.”

"Gardening, yoga, meditation, and I still want to slap someone!"

Only dull people are lively in the mornings.

Laugh, and the world laughs with you…

…snore, and you sleep alone.

If you haven't got
anything nice to say,
come and sit by me.

If you haven't
got anything nice to say…
be vague…

You'll always
pick up more dirt
with a phone than
with a hoover.

Start each day with a smile
and get it over with.

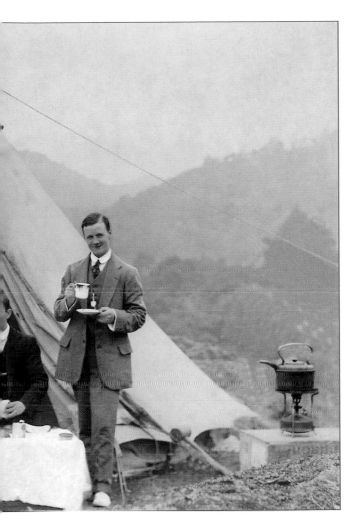

With a cup of tea in your hand, anything is possible.

Some friends tell all.

Some friends' lips are sealed.

Will you be my Facebook friend?

"Eat up dear, then you can tweet all your friends what you had for breakfast."

"Get in touch,
or we'll come and visit."

If you're not annoying the
neighbours you're listening
to the wrong music.

God sees everything,
but the neighbours
miss nothing.

Under no circumstances
should one forget
one's manners.

Here we are: powerful, erotic and ready to go.

You drink, swear and have questionable morals. You're everything I want in a friend.

Nothing beats
a wild night out
with the girls.

If you're not
embarrassing your
children, you're probably
not enjoying yourself.

"You can drive,
    I've got to drink."

"I like my parties cool and my friends hot."

"I like my parties hot and my friends cool."

The donkey dreaded
hen parties.

Husbands come and go, but friends are forever.

Once you realise
we are all mad, life starts
to make sense.

Get some friends.

Before you need them.

"You'll always
be my friend.
You know too much
about me."

If I ain't got friends,
then I ain't nothing.

Cath Tate has lived and worked in London for more years than she cares to mention. She currently runs a greeting card company, Cath Tate Cards, with her daughter Rosie: the bulk of the photos and captions in this book started life as greetings cards.

The photos have been collected over the years by Cath and her friends in junk shops and vintage fairs. They are all genuine and show people in all their glory, on the beach, on a day out, posing stiffly for the photographer, drinking with friends, smiling or scowling at the camera.

The photographs were all taken sometime between 1880 and 1960. Times change but people, their friendships, their little joys and stupid mistakes, remain the same. Some things have changed though, and Cath Tate has used modern technical wizardry to tease some colour into the cheeks of those whose cheeks lost their colour some time ago.

The quotes that go with the photos come from random corners of life and usually reflect some current concern that is bugging her.

If you want to see all the current greetings cards and other ephemera available from Cath Tate Cards see www.cathtatecards.com

Cath Tate

Many thanks to all those helped me put this book together, including Discordia, who have fed me with wonderful photos and ideas over the years, and Suzanne Perkins, who has made sure everything looks OK, and also has a good line in jokes.

Picture credits

Photos from the collection of Cath Tate apart from the following:
Discordia/Simon: Pages 4–5, 6–7, 40–41, 44–45, 46–47, 50–51, 64–65, 72–73, 84–85, 88–89, 94–5
Discordia/Kulturrecycling: Pages 10–11, 86–87, 92–93, 106–107
Discordia/Siegmann: Pages 38–39, 82–83,
Keith Allen: Pages 14–15
Marianne Kerlinski: Pages 108–109